WANDERING

Selected Poems

(from the past fifty years)

by Michael L. Newell

Acknowledgements

Many of these poems (sometimes in a different form) have previously appeared in the following periodicals, to whose editors grateful acknowledgement is made: *Aethlon: The Journal of Sports Literature*; *Alpha Beat Press*; *Asylum*; *Bakunin*; *Bellowing Ark*; *Black Poppy Review*; *The Blind Man's Rainbow*; *Carpe Laureate Diem*; *City Primeval*; *College English*; *Comstock Review*; *Culture Counter*; *Current*; *English Journal*; *Etcetera*; *First Class*; *FortyOunceBachelor*; *The Higginsville Reader*; *The Iconoclast*; *Jerry Jazz Musician*; *KSOR Guide to the Arts*; *Lilliput Review*; *Little Eagle's Re/Verse*; *Lucid Moon*; *Main Street Rag Poetry Journal*; *Mandrake*; *MM Review*; *Muse of Fire*; *Northridge Review*; *The Plastic Tower*; *Poetry Depth Quarterly*; *Poetry/LA*; *Poppy Road Review*; *Potpourri*; *Riverrun*; *Shemom*; *Ship of Fools*; *Tucumcari Literary Review*; and *Verse-Virtual*.

Some Previous Books and Chapbooks by Michael L. Newell

Kindling	(Wayfaring Stranger Press, 1991)
Cradle Song	(Wayfaring Stranger Press, 1992)
Empty Theatres	(Wayfaring Stranger Press, 1996)
A Stranger to the Land	(Garden Street Press, 1997)
School Metaphors	(Lockout Press, 2002)
There's An End to It	(Lockout Press, 2002)
Long Gores Suite	(Lockout Press), 2002)
Miles of Highways and Open Roads	(Four Sep Publications, 1999)
Collision Course	(Four Sep Publications, 1999)
Seeking Shelter	(Four Sep Publications, 2004)
A Parcel of Rogues	(Four Sep Publications, 2004)
A Long Time Traveling	(Four Sep Publications, 2004)
Traveling without Compass or Map	(Bellowing Ark Press, 2006)
Meditation of an Old Man Standing on a Bridge	(Bellowing Ark Press, 2018)

Acknowledgements (page two)

"Golden" first appeared in *English Journal*, Vol. 85, No. 8 (December, 1996), p.65, copyright 1996, by the National Council of Teachers of English. Printed by their permission.

"For James Edmondson as Willy Loman" first appeared in *College English*, September 1993, copyright 1993, by the National Council of Teachers of English. Printed by their permission.

I would like to thank Anna and Michael Citrino (for many years of support for my work); I am also grateful to fellow poets and generous readers of many of my poems over an extended period of time: Dan Franch, Michael Minassian, Ed Ruzicka, and the indomitable, witty, self-effacing Robert Wexelblatt.

I also want to say thank you to a handful of small press editors who have helped me greatly over the years: Robert R. Ward, Don Wentworth, Joe Maita, Phil Wagner, Jack Hart, and Firestone Feinberg.

Cover Photography: Michael Citrino

TABLE OF CONTENTS

I. THE CHARACTER OF HATS

(Poems from 1971-1989)

TABLE OF CONTENTS (page two)

II. THAT HAND WHICH WAS NEVER WITHDRAWN

(Poems from 1990-2005)

TABLE OF CONTENTS (page three)

III. OF GOODBYES MEMORIES AND EIDOLONS

(Poems from 2006-2020)

This book is dedicated to my siblings: David,

Brian, Ruth, Patrick, Donald, Peter, and

Robert who all have been generous in their

support of my work as a poet, and who have

always forgiven my many eccentricities.

The Character of Hats:

Poems from 1971 - 1989

GIFT

in a corner
dusty as an unstrung guitar
by a window
where wind fills cracks

> strand round strand
> as arms round others
> the bamboo stool you gave
> quietly comes undone

> (Northridge, California, 1971)

EYELIFTED MOONHIGH: AN INCANTATION

"Yellow me, moongold;
          starwarm, shower me;
              flower me, Aurora Borealis."

A boon:

lust me skyward,
          boybelly-gleeful,
             night bound,
                wound in black,

receive me back, Childhood;

trek me boyjourneys,
          blackberry-packed
             in battle mock,
                wounded laserly.

"Tattle me not to mother or father;
  farther brothers soar we in summer dark than ever they."

Stumbled time bruises me,
         worries me old in flesh
             no wine can cure nor age reclaim.

Bearfooted,
      lumbering,
         slumberheaded,

eyes scaled with middling years--

for tonight,
"Yellow me, moongold;
          starwarm, shower me;
              flower me, Aurora Borealis."

Boon me this
second

Childhood.

(Northridge, California, 1972)

THE CHARACTER OF HATS

A hat properly aged
releases the fisherman
cast inside a steel worker,

the dancer shimmering
in an accountant's figures,
the sailor deep

inside a coal miner,
the woodsman wandering
in a priest.

*****

A hat aged properly,
stiffness mellowed into character,
smells of salt water

brine pickling skin, rain
streaming through Douglas Fir, firewood
kindling friendships, pipes

lit from embers
warming conversation, contains
sun, earth, tree, fire, rain, and moon.

(Mission Hills, California, 1972)

YANKEE TRADER
(for Nehemiah W. Newell)

At ten he worked
his dad's lobster smack.

The Great Depression rolled across Yarmouth.
Steam replaced sail in the fishing fleet.
His dad warped and buckled.

He was self-sufficient at thirteen.

Together with Peggy he raised eight kids, Cape Cod
to Yokohama; sometimes tangled in their arms and legs,
a fleshy seaweed.

Squalls racing gulls over waves
in sleep
would turn into midnight toothaches
                       three a.m. colic
                         nightmares.

He says,
        "All my life I've supported others;
        now I need to be alone with my wife."

Touching her
        sails release.
They blossom in the night.

(Mission Hills, California, 1976)

THURSDAY I DECIDED TO GIVE UP ACTING

I fell asleep and dreamed I was a master weaver.
A factory grew outside my window and I smashed
my loom to kindling. Rain bleared the window
as I tossed fire upon the rubble.

I woke sobbing, not knowing where I was
or what I wept for. Wind cradled my apartment.
The rooms rocked in a careless rhythm.

All afternoon I read and rain fell
through a widening crack in the living room ceiling.
When Carol came home from work that night, she asked,
"Michael, Michael, why didn't you put buckets under
            the leak?"

I sipped cocoa and continued to read Godot. She stood
behind me and wrapped her arms round my neck.
I released myself, walked outside on the back porch stairs,
and watched thick swirling clouds half-lit by moonlight
as they rode past like waves, like time, like dreams
muddied by life. I imagined black smoke disturbing
            the night.

"Tomorrow I hunt for a real job."
I shivered, pulled my Pendleton tighter.
Carol called through the window,
"Would you mind walking the dog? She needs to go out."

I couldn't move.
Runoff from the rain shook the roof
drainpipe and splattered my face. The moon
vanished. A plate shattered in the kitchen.
"Damn, damn, damn."

(Van Nuys, California, 1978)

THREE OLD LADIES LUNCHING

their voices float
among potted plants

forks pry open
cold clams artichokes and families

each bite hangs
in the air
a dilemma

coffee is served
and thin blue hair
fills
        with rising steam

(Universal City, California, 1979)

HER NAME IS

seven sons and a daughter four more born dead
one dress for church one pair of pants
to scrub trailer floors and clothes in boiled well water
flash cards to drill her children in reading and math
aged and retarded cradled as her own
brightest student in her high school and college
hours daily before a stove kneading and forming leftovers
the child who spoke only her name
clinging for hours to become the family's best mind
her potter's wheel shaping clay like so many lives
alone in a trailer with kids her husband at sea for years
mumps measles mono chicken pox poison ivy hives
survived Mark Twain read aloud seven kinds of homemade
bread and religion thrived best in private
no one told her how much they cared
suicide prevented by children afraid to lose life itself
don't know her never did but this
is a thank you note a son's naming

(Van Nuys, California, 1979)

THE MAN WITH THE GLASS HEAD

I. The Humdrum Blues

Someone is always painting
him--he ends up gray.

*

He brushes on five o'clock
shadow so people won't think
he can't grow hair.

*

A girl draws a heart on his face,
fills it with their initials.
He's seen tapdancing.

Later he holds a hammer lightly,
tests it on his head. She walks away.
He throws it where she was standing.

*

Daydreaming,
the problem is peeping toms.
Curtains help. Smoggy or rainy days help.
Or sitting high in a tree.

II. He Visits His Hometown

Old Mr. Williams still finds it funny
to spray him with tobacco juice,
wash it off with a hose.
The old man laughs and his teeth tumble
out and are lost in the weeds.

A former teacher says you look familiar,
but it's hard to tell
one glass head from another.

Streets have shrunk and sun
filling his head makes him shake violently.
He puts on a hat to avoid
starting fires.

In his motel room he goes blind,
frosted over by the air conditioner.

On the Greyhound home,
smoke litters seats and aisles.
Highways and tinted windows blot the past.
He flicks ashes from teeth,
pretends to read or sleep.
Thoughts settle
like soot.

(Van Nuys, California 1980)

TOWNS ON HILLS

I know the feel of towns on hills,
sad as fairy tales.

I've felt their air before:
wind wrapping autumn streets in leaves,
people crossing red lights haloed and sweating
in chill Puget fog.

In a hillside deserted park,
a windblown rain-rusted merry-go-round --
my father runs pushing four sons a daughter
in the shadow of a Catholic church.

*

I forget why I'm here, that tomorrow I leave:
sixteen hours by Greyhound to L.A.,

longing for the hook-handed man across the aisle
with his red-white-and-blue tattoo
to put out his cigarette
so I can sleep.

(Ashland, Oregon, 1980)

5:45 A.M.

Rain has knit three days together.

> "What the hell
> I'll take a walk."

Across the valley, fields
throb with green, cows dot
low clouds in the hollows
and ravines on hillsides.

Streets are swarming: slugs, worms, birds breakfasting,
dogs and a jogger -- their breath a geyser
of steam, a drunk rummaging
behind The Log Cabin Tavern, a lone police car --
the driver's glasses steamed from coffee, a Greyhound
headed for Vancouver -- window faces
vague as the Siskiyous behind a cloudbank.

I dampen in the slow rain.
My hat comes off, shirt opens,
face tilts up; I could hear
a snail crawl.

My breath flows
with the rhythm of waters.

When I go home into sleep,
I float
on creeks threading farms.

(Ashland, Oregon, Spring 1981)

EARLY SUMMER DAY

A dog sits in a breeze. Smells and sounds
float through her body, fur rippling.

The steady sun presses eyelids shut, deepens
the center of the valley, whole families
swallowed unresisting.

*

Overhead a bamboo kite
rests between clouds.

Shade from my door drapes me. Movement
seems ponderous. Suddenly I am sprayed
by an unseen sprinkler.
My hands twist slowly, water-seeking tendrils.
My body lengthens through the yard.

(Ashland, Oregon, Spring 1981)

THE INTRUDER

Writing this I feel a chill.
I say it's the night air. I say it's the fan.
I avoid the door.
I'm grateful the dog sleeps and senses nothing.
I leave all the cottage lights on...

A creaking late at night.
I cautiously went to the door, looked out
at the darkened porch. He stood there,
bushy-bearded, hollow-eyed, shoulder-length hair spilling
across reddened cheeks and nose, staring at me.
I started to scream --
then recognized my reflection. I tried to laugh
and went to bed.

Sirens fill the night. Carol shouts
in her sleep, the broom crashes
to the floor, and ants trek
across the ceiling.

I came here a refugee
from cities, but outside is something
I brought with me. When I touch Carol,
she shivers and reaches for cover.

(Ashland, Oregon, Summer 1981)

FOR JAMES EDMONDSON AS WILLY LOMAN
(The Oregon Shakespeare Festival, 1981)

Before anyone arrives,
he's backstage with suitcases
dreaming a past.

In dressing room mirror, a clock
for his face. His fingers delicately adjust the hands.
He pulls on clothes, pulls up shoulders
so head can shrink into them, steps
out of time. His eyes fill with ashes.

The father has planted dreams tougher than weeds
in cavities of sons. Brush fires are raging.
The father dies, a burst of light.
When he is boarded up and laid to rest,
every voice says a different name.

During curtain call, the actor begins fumbling
back toward time. He speaks in whispers
(voice tucked away with other props)
and won't look in mirrors. His skull
gleams through skin, a slowly cooling
blue heat. He won't sleep for hours.

Trying to climb back into his body,
nothing fits.

(Ashland, Oregon, 1981)

**AT THE ASHLAND OREGON OLD TIME
FIDDLERS' CONCERT**

While Sara Kaye fiddled
on Independence Day in Lithia Park,
a black swallowtail butterfly went mad

tracing music in the air: the opening
and closing of wings, the furling
and unfurling of notes.

(Ashland, Oregon, Summer 1981)

THE FIDDLE

remembers the forest, the wind's varied strokes
sounding branches through the deep well of years.
It sings with the throats of sparrow, hawk, and owl.
Deep inside its body dwell shadows
of moon, leaf, and bark. Its past
haunts all its melodies, caged
in a city, a room, a leather case.
No one yet has learned its secret name.
It laments with the bitter edge of the exile.

(Los Angeles, 1982)

VINTAGE INN, ASHLAND, OREGON (4/16/81)
(for The PJQ Quintet)

Trumpet and Voice roam together
                    Sax gusts above
Piano Keys
                    spill and tumble (a mountain creek
or lover filled with abandon)   Love Her   raps Drum

ice cubes swing
                    rattle

                        sway
                            floorboards dance
                            CRAZY
                                a cartoon

every marriage needs witnesses and we nod
clap our hands   stomp our feet   such noisy guests
a wonder we're allowed to stay

silence tightens breathing
we wonder if more's to come...

tipping the waiter we imagine
a collection for lovers
and grin foolishly

outside the night is filled
with cigarette smoke   lightning
and Lithia Creek swirling over rocks
and wooden supports of the Vintage Inn

we sit on our car's hood for hours
with friends
                we pretend
we're a traveling band   our hands
shape imaginary notes

ah love love crazy love   nothing quite like it
for igniting the blood   you and I are muted trumpet
softly singing of night and day   swirling sax celebrating
what is and is to come   sensuous guitar and rippling piano
all suggestive of what could be   all suggesting the night
is ours   and the wind whispers of the hours to come

(Ashland, Oregon, 4/16/1981)

LATE JULY IN SIMI VALLEY

Dusk. I walk to a field, sit
on a low hill, my dog breathing
on my knee, and settle deep into grass;

two bats veer past; a few small
scattered trees blend into night;
my dog sleeps and the air cools

to a dream: I'm a boy sitting
in Cranberry Lake shallows
amidst a cadence of crickets.

Behind me through the fence, lawn chairs
rust in oil-scarred driveways.
Distant houses submerge, a wavering blue haze

broken by flashes like electric eels.
Soon sprinklers will turn on, driving me back.
For now, I hum along with my dog's soft snoring.

(Simi Valley, California, Summer 1982)

GALE FORCE

"I can no longer tolerate this room
with its smells of you and me together
only distance and time can cleanse me"

I remember rain slamming against glass
washing the last snow away
I wanted to open the window and let it
flood the room

                    give you what you wanted
                    or was it me who wanted

wind flooded the central heater
banging whistling filling walls with fear
anger made physical and we stared at intimate
objects seeing only each other while looking
in separate directions

night was rising strong as the storm
yet we left lights on even as we finally slept
side by side without touching

in my dreams blank walls
bled shadows

                    a hoarse voice kept asking

                    "what have we done
                        have we done"

some echoes never fully fade
some winds blow forever

        (Shawnee, Kansas, 1983)

SEPARATING

When you say, "I'm leaving,"
and begin to sob,

I feel a strange elation,
not for your departure,
but for your crumpled face.

I say, "Stay, stay,"
and press you tight;
I am a child squeezing
hot laundry to his face.

                    *

Amputees still feel
severed limbs--

how long will my left arm
remember your weight?

                    (Kansas City, Kansas, 1983)

NANCY

and no one can know
your heart that secret
stone you letter alone at midnight

stroking your hair listening
your breathing deep sleep
I hear sounds that raise

neck hairs you half-sob half-snarl
fingers claw your pillow
the house is frail as rice paper

the old setter stares blindly
my fingers gingerly
brush your hair

(Van Nuys, California, 1985)

A HAND HALF-RAISED

(for Hitomi Murakami)

tonight clouds
row across the moon
propelled by dark oars

a curtain of fine rain
is draped from the balcony

on a phonograph nearby
a shakuhachi mourns

the apartment next door
stands cruelly open
emptied of all its kindness

Murakami-san has returned to Japan

the rain stitches my grief
onto the huge sleeve of uncaring
night

(North Hollywood, California, 1987)

NOW AND THEN

A breeze strokes the skin of a pool;
a dog licks herself slowly;
a cloud absentmindedly drapes the moon;

soon we are upstairs;
the long slow rhythm of search, blessed
stillness, we find how breathing

makes quilts float through a room, how
fingers become incandescent -- a colony of fireflies;
when the rain starts, we listen

for hours -- now and then
one of us says, "Don't
leave, never leave." Now

and then I remember these things,
lying alone as the wind slams
sheets of rain through the screen,

as my fingers turn gray under lamplight,
as the room darkens and shadows
stream down walls.

                    (Van Nuys, California, 1987)

THE PACKRAT

No never no never no
never again cried the bent man to the wind--
never again will I dance to the fiddle
that filled my spring days with leaps, shouts, and laughter;

my back crooks, a question mark
shaped like life, my fumbling life
that stumbles through alleys, down piers,
beneath rotting bridges where children's voices
peal out: look at the funny fat gray bearded man
tripping over his bellbottoms, his seedy old bellbottoms;

I pass lovers, my hungry eyes averted from their shrinking;
I pass lovers, my ears keen for every sound of passion,
scraps to feed on as darkness falls, as I creep under bushes
or trash bins, as my voice fondles swatches of melody
from boyhood, when wind sang of flight into perpetual sun
and the moon and stars were a gem-studded shawl;

I pass lovers and stuff the pockets of my heart
with others' dreams to be sorted through greedily--
I know somewhere in these volumes I cart about
is a life I might have lived;
now even fresh-fallen snow blackens beneath swollen feet
wrapped in rags discarded by the profligate young;

to see only others, or the past, is my motto
as I huddle in the undemanding company of broken bottles,
tin cans, and the mind's ashes...

(Van Nuys, California, 1988)

THE POET

(for Robert Bly)

It was the face within the face
that caught my eye. It was
the lips hidden deep within the cheek
that moved in their own buried time
speaking silent lines that rang
throughout a crowded hall calling,
"Listen listen listen. No one needs
ears or words to hear my music; no one
needs eyes to read my lips. All you need
is a heart and mind able to be still,
to breathe without utterance of sound,
to be so unutterably quiet that you can feel
a moth's wings stir the air beyond the locked window."

For one terrifying second I saw his flesh
dissolve and heard the clacking of bone
on grinning bone. I heard the eternal tone
we all will know alone in unknown space.
I groaned with the agony of a wounded animal
and the moment passed. It was just a hall filled
with people politely listening to words politely
uttered into a microphone.
No drama, no momentous occasion. Just a reading
of an ordinary poet's ordinary words.

(Van Nuys, California, Autumn 1989)

35

**That Hand Which Was Never Withdrawn:
Poems from 1990 - 2005**

SPRING ARRIVES

I stand in a freshly plowed field at night,
inhale the rich incense released by earth,
and cup hands to catch trickles of starlight.
My feet sprout roots, bones swell until they burst
through skin and unfurl branches left and right.
Wind rises. The moon blossoms and gives birth
to choirs of insects serenading night.
Sparrows light, snuggle in my leaves for warmth.

Couples in nearby homes sleepily bury
faces in the soft leaves of lovers' hair.
Everywhere the seeds of hope are ferried
by the night wind with calm parental care.
Everywhere grasses and flowers revive;
summoned by sun, wind, and rain, the new crops thrive.

(Khilda, Amman, Jordan, 1993)

GOLDEN

Outside Amman, burnished
by the last light of day: fields,
hills, sky, and distant skyline of city buildings
rim the edge of vision. Move your head
quickly and the world flames in a golden dance.

The evening is rich with light, so rich
it could be mined if you could
find tools fine enough to filter
particles immersed in air. A simple breath
is weighted with rare luxury.

(Jordan, Autumn 1992)

SAVE THE LAST DANCE FOR ME

Ah, the Drifters in full voice
and I'm seventeen--standing
and watching, always
watching while others carom
lightly through the steps,
those beautiful, awful twists
and turns where the young
find the doors to the world,
glide through and find
themselves forty with three kids,
a serious job, a house with car,
swimming pool, t.v. set,
and a spouse still dancing, only
now the steps of each
leave deep imprints on the floor
and ignore the direction of the other.

And I, I'm still back outside that first door;
I never did find a way to join the dance
that ushered my friends into the world.
The faint music of memory steadily dims,
my chest constricts, and all life
whirls past--jostling, tumbling,
turning, rude, noisy, and painful--
as I stand and watch untouched,
unseen, forgotten, still
trying to learn the words to the damn song,
trying to execute a few simple steps.

(Khilda, Amman, Jordan 1992-1993)

RECIDIVIST

A flower splits
unyielding concrete

and your smile
gently nudges

its way into
my harsh thoughts;

ah, the weeds
of love--

they lunch on stone
and metal

and infuse scrapyards
with life's colors.

(Amman, Jordan, 1993)

POSTCARDS FROM ABU DHABI
(the United Arab Emirates, 1993-1995)

1.

So many veiled women here,
draped like trees
enveloped in twilight,
rain, and fog.

2.

Robes of men (from Egypt, Afghanistan,
the Sudan) sweep the earth, floating
to and from the mosque, brushing
aside autos, suits, hotel bars, Pizza Huts.

3.

For an hour this morning, rain
fell, the first in nearly a year,
sand deepening in color, streets
and children in wild disarray.

4.

To be alone here
is to be like fog
with nothing to curl around
or brush against.

5.

So many trees, so much grass,
on a desert island,
paid for by charred skies: Los Angeles,
Bangkok, Denver, Phoenix, Tokyo.

6.

Night sky is high above
unless you look down at surrounding sea,
and there it is -- planets, stars, and, ah,
bright love, its long throat trumpeting over waves.

(Abu Dhabi, UAE, 1993-1995)

HARRY LOST IN THE RIBALD WIND

Ah, the carelessness of wind
creating love, a salad
of tossed hair and blown clothing;

the tang of imagination
dresses the whole affair,
addresses exchanged in mind
only, mine not really
mine, nor would hers be
hers, nor would we
be what the wind
so casually suggests
we are, nor are we ever
what the wind would
lead us to believe;

and yet still we follow,
one fine gust after another,
love after love, alone
with the wind
and imagination...

(Abu Dhabi, 1994)

HARRY AT THE PARK

Today the trees
in constant motion, you've
seen the same thing
at cocktail parties, in restaurants,
on the beach, bodies
moving to the breath
of the world, do wop,
classical, and jazz;

and all afternoon, I hung
around the park
listening to the clear
running water of eucalyptus
in full swing and sway,
imagining a tenor sax in
the hands of say, Coleman Hawkins,
jamming with the wind and leaves.

(Khilda, Amman, Jordan, Spring 1993)

HARRY DEFINES INTIMACY

To brush a crumb off
the corner of a mouth,
to adjust a strand
of hair, to casually
tilt your head to accept
such gestures.
To think nothing of the exchange.

(Abu Dhabi, Autumn 1993)

LEAVING YOKOHAMA
(for Tetsuo "Ted" Kanamori)

Twelve and frantic, I wanted
to find Tetsuo, tell him goodbye;
but we were already packed
and then we were on the bus

driving through American military housing
on the way to the harbor
and the long trip home.
We were passing a field

filled with boys playing baseball
and the ball floated towards
left field. I could nearly smell
the leather of the glove that nabbed it,

deprived it of air, and suddenly realized
the fielder firing the ball back to shortstop
was Tetsuo. I tried to open a window,
but it was sealed shut; the air

conditioned bus was built with childproof windows;
I felt hot, I couldn't breathe,
I felt squeezed like a ball in leather;
I tasted salt and felt

my father slip an arm
round my shoulders and explain
why we couldn't stop. On the receding field
Tetsuo was trotting to the dugout. His side was up.

Thirty-five years later I still
hate windows that won't open.
And when I see a ball suspended above
an outfielder, I want to yell a warning.

(Abu Dhabi, 1993)

THAT HAND WHICH WAS NEVER WITHDRAWN

Night torn apart, my mother storming out the trailer,
my father trying to comfort four terrified children
who blamed him -- not understanding poverty maims
even the kindest hearts. Eventually my mother returned
and my parents clung, each to the other, for hours.
I, ten, cursed my father till I slept.

Next day after school my father waited
with the old Willy's jeep to pick me up. I cursed
him again, slapped away his encircling arm. Silence.

"We must talk sooner or later." His voice
was barely audible. "I hate you," I said. "I hate you
and will never talk to you again." I glanced at him:
his face caved in, his eyes lost down the country road.
His voice floated up from some deep cavern or well
where people go when pain is too great for daylight.

"Michael, you will be my son for years. No matter
what you say or do, you will always be my son.
And I love you." I looked out the window in disgust.

Thirty-six years later, eight thousand miles from home,
I stare at the rare sight of rain falling
on the sands of Abu Dhabi.
Next door parents and children scream in Arabic
and the universal language of pain. I reach
for that hand which was never withdrawn. I find
only damp air and oceans between us.

(Abu Dhabi, 1991)

MY PARENTS PHONE ME OVERSEAS

In the backyard
a waterfall

visited over and over
by a hummingbird

it can't get enough
nor can my mother

watching from the porch
with the same fascination

as my father watches
them both

the flowers around
the yard exuberant

and so am I
listening on the phone

awash in gladiolus, hummingbirds,
waterfalls, parents, and

a midnight array of stars
above my balcony

(Abu Dhabi, 1994)

CRADLE SONG

Once again the wind embraces fields, rough
arms shaking grass, bush, and tree,
an arrogant grip reminiscent of a father
tossing a child higher, higher before a saving
catch sure and full of coarse affection.

I remember flight out of and into my own
father's arms, and my own bearish handling
of flights for younger brothers and sister,
and they lift their sons and daughters
in excited flight, generations soaring;

and the wind wraps night
in an awkward tender grip
and rocks us all to sleep:

father brother sister mother tree bush stone…

(Abu Dhabi, 1991)

A MEMORY OF WATER

Rain rips through the night
in savage gusts, tattoos
the window which sighs, punch-drunk,
a fighter about to topple.

I roll over in bed, deep
contentment, snug, dry,
remembering a hundred other times
I have sprawled like this, listening
to drumming on roof and window.

The shadow filling the room
is bigger than night or memory
and I slide into it, a familiar robe--
warm, worn, comforting.

There is a history here, yours and mine,
a chronicle of cells growing more complex,
moving toward dry land but never
forgetting, always coming back to the shore to dangle
a foot, a toe, a sleepy lolling around

the edge of water--
like tonight as I leave
a window half-opened
and turn my face to the fine spray.

(Khilda, Amman, Jordan, Spring 1993)

SOON

Rows of students grimly scribbling, neatly
uniformed; they know they must
PAY ATTENTION TOMORROW IS THE TEST!

What about the day after tomorrow
and the day after that?
Another test? And another?

Soon they will be tested on whether
they can have children or marriages
that last or jobs spent scribbling in rows;

soon they will have grandchildren
in rows scribbling, neat
in their uniforms;

soon they will be uniformly in rows
laid beneath stone and earth
with scribbling on the stone;

soon there will be only the stone
with the wind scribbling; soon
there will be only the wind;

soon...
he thought
and scribbled.

(Amman, Jordan, 1992-1993)

ANNUNCIATION

Through a window
spring arrives, perches
first on the sill --
trilling the song of flowers;
then visits the chandelier,
dusty yellowed fixtures
brighter for her song of light;
the bedroom next, unkempt
and shabby as my wintry soul,
straightens and freshens --
blessed by her song of breeze and shade;
I lie on the couch and listen --
all through the neighborhood
children have come out to greet her;
when she goes to meet them,
her songs blend with sunlight
mottled by new leaves
throwing a mosaic of hope
across the room.

(Amman, Jordan, Spring 1993)

WRONG NUMBERS

Always an unknown language
and a stranger's voice,

the past arriving with an unfamiliar
sound and shape,

the future pounding on the door, ringing the bell,
the police, the Ministry of Who Are You,

the neighbor prying into your secrets,
three ex-lovers and a lost and angry friend,

let all the bells ring unanswered -- not one
signals a rocking chair, a warm blanket, an embrace.

(Tashkent, Uzbekistan, 1997)

MAILBOX

Open the lid
and the wind
howls across continents.

Twigs sometimes appear
with a brown leaf or two
which I study for clues.

Last week a butterfly
emerged, lit on my left ear.
I failed to decode its flapping.

I awoke today to a roaring
like a hurricane at sea -- my hands
tremble and refuse to open the box.

(Tashkent, Uzbekistan, 1997)

TWO TAKE ROOT

I.
A cottonwood seed armada
sails an evening Tashkent wind.

It glides and bobs past sycamore,
white oak, an assembly

of ballet-goers, two shabby
drunks, and a crippled beggar

who uses her one gnarled
hand to touch passersby.

People flick her hand away
almost absent-mindedly,

the way they brush the seeds
out of their eyes and hair.

II.
In Tashkent's impoverished economic soil,
beggars sprout everywhere--

human weeds in abandoned
asphalt lots.

Every annoyed hand
which flicks the poor aside

clones a dozen more beggars
with the stunned eyes

of clubbed fish
gasping for air.

Grasping for cash, leftover scraps
of bread, discarded slices of pizza,

half-eaten chicken bones, cheap vodka,
staggering in the wake of the well-

dressed, the financially fit, the survivors
of an economic wasteland, these are

the whisperers, the ghost
voices on night's wind, dead cells

society sheds which refuse
to disappear or absolve us.

III.
The cottonwood seeds sink taproots
into Tashkent's oasis water.

The poor multiply even faster
in Tashkent's economic desert,

a twentieth century version
of the miracle of loaves and fishes,

a feast featuring the starving elderly,
child beggars, and teenage prostitutes:

Mary Magdalenes whose Christs
are fat European and American businessmen,

and the apostles and disciples are minor
corporate or government functionaries

who busily crunch between their teeth
the seeds carelessly strewn by their leaders.

Nothing can grow where scavengers
pillage every crumb, seed, and dropping.

(Tashkent, Uzbekistan, 1998)

DIDDLEY-BOP-SHE-BOP

Them knees,
full of bees again,

two gates
flapping in a stuttering breeze,

hands rapping
tables, thighs,

high up on
the chest, invest

the body in
the bopping sound

of Mister Monk
doing the Bemsha Swing,

the funkiest thing
in town tonight,

an old tape
lighting up Tashkent.

Swing that thing.
Make these rainy streets

ring in Navruz,
Central Asian New Year.

(At The Cafe in Tashkent, Uzbekistan, Monk on the box,
1998)

**THOUGHTS ON A THEME OF JAMES ASHBROOK
PERKINS**

"Hawks do not sing"

Yet when they take wing,
their brute mastery of air

turns the universe up
or down or steady level

as they need. Having
only needs, never desires,

they need not sing -- song
being the rush of whim, fancy, hope,

despair, prayer, and wild surmise.
A scream suffices for creatures

which are all need or satiety.
Perfect engines for survival, they have no need

for music or poetry -- there are
no spaces to be filled in them.

"Music is the food of life" only
when the imagination can grasp

the concept of loss
gnawing at the heart for decades,

or an ocean rolling
across the sun's path in memory.

Song is a survival trait only
when mere survival is insufficient.

(Tashkent, Uzbekistan, 1998)

PSALM IN A RAINSTORM

If the wind is your father
slamming you against a wall
to ensure you listen,

if the ocean is God
encircling, watching,
sustaining life,

if the mountain is
your obdurate self
blocking your own way,

then the rain is mother
to us all, bathing us in tears --
long rippling fingers of forgiveness

and hope.

(Long Gores, Norfolk, England, July 1998)

PERCHANCE TO DREAM

In the living arms
        of women and trees,
                in the great breathing

which girdles the globe,
        in the immense womb
                which spawns all life,

sink, sink, sink,
        towards the drifting
                which comes with sleep,

the floating just beneath
        the surface where the mind
                becomes a leaf loose in the universe,

where tumbling twisting turning,
        all yearning (for knowledge, for change,
                for stasis) merges,

and the sky holds all prayer
        the earth all passion
                and the sea rocks and croons,

rocks and croons, and our mouths,
        soundless, open and close, open
                and close, in dumb amazement.

(Long Gores, Norfolk, England, July 1998)

TALKING TO MY STUDENTS

Words stream through my mouth, a channel
for voices I had forgotten: there's my father,
how did he get in there--I thought I had left
him at the ancestral home and moved myself
on down the road; there's old Bob lecturing
my drama class--why the sneaky bastard even
slips into my English classes where he has no
territorial rights; Ben, dead and buried, brings
his ascetic haunted face and voice, his moral
clarity, into my discussions--softly scolding
my lack of rigor; singing a song, there is Joseph
smiling, nodding encouragement, making sure
I keep time accurately, hit the right notes,
remember the melody, treat the lyrics with respect;
I have become a river where streams merge--dozens
of friends, teachers, relatives, colleagues, students,
even an occasional enemy, have filled me
with their thoughts, their words, their rhythms; I am
a typical American, mongrel to the core, never one,
always many, never pure, always a mixture
of contradictory traits which strengthen one another;
my current carries with it the debris of every life
which has brushed up against me; my voice, I tell
the faces in front of me, is not my own, it belongs
to every person I have known; it belongs to you.

(Cairo, Egypt, 2002)

ESTRANGEMENT

I have lived so long among strangers
that I have become strange to myself.

Each step I take is weighted with memory.
Each window I pass reflects a stranger--

strange how each face is strangely familiar
in each strange place.

When I return home where memory resides,
the familiar has grown strange.

The wind blows from a different direction,
there are ruined buildings on familiar corners,

the newspaper has changed its name,
and there is a new minister in the old church

who wears his father's face
with some unexpected alterations.

The river is half its former size;
the town barely survives.

In strange lands where no one knows me,
and on streets I have known all my life,

the strange has grown oddly familiar,
and the familiar oddly strange.

Cairo, Egypt, 2001-2002

CHALLENGE

rascal depths the life I lead
he winked and stripped a wallet
from a passing pedestrian

nonsense that life over there
he flicked his head toward
a distant brace of skyscrapers

inhaling and exhaling a stream
of three piece suits and
swaying mini-skirts

I might have been those you know
then laughed naw not me I need
the challenge of laws to slip

between around under and over
what is the point of order
without subversion

I slum among the gentry to do
what I was born to do but I live
in darkest alley and meanest club

this interview is over slip back where
you came from before I remove
all you value and hide from scrutiny

at last sight of him he was waving one hand
over his head while the other tipped
bourbon to his smirking lips

eyes in the walls directed me
out a gate into the world beyond
his rascal depths and I relaxed

in sunshine poured from a blue pitcher
and celebrated the order of daylight
dipped into a pocket my hand

discovered all notes all my documents
were gone gone gone vanished
in the chaos I had just left

midnight a phone call you can have them
all you need do is return and claim them
no safe conduct this time you must take

your chances you must meet me razor
to eye blade to throat you must be willing
to reinvent yourself and all you know...

(Tallinn, Estonia, Autumn 2002)

DANCING FROM MEMORY

all afternoon the wind
blew whatever was available
(leaf, hat, gown, scarf, coat,
candy bar wrapper, beer can)
in a fandango of breath and
whirling movement his partners
changing from one minute
to the next a swirl of color
and shape filling his outdoor stage

one old woman speared her flying
hat with her cane and deftly spun it
round and back into her hand
before tying it onto her head
one would have sworn her cane
tapped a flamenco beat as she
strolled off to a nearby bus stop
her stride (perhaps hard to believe)
radiated a sultry insouciance

waiting for her bus she swayed
to some rhythm older than her bones
the wind lightly lifted her gown
then gracefully redraped it round
her swing and sway swing and sway
her eyes were shut her lips seemed
to whisper words only she could hear
who knows what year she was revisiting
who it was her arms reached toward

(Tallinn, Estonia, Spring 2003)

67

DIRECTIONALLY CHALLENGED

I move forward into the world,
my tweed cap jauntily cocked
to duplicate the optimistic bounce in my step
and the aggressive roll and thrust of my shoulders.

Suddenly the wind lifts my cap, casually
flings it behind me. I turn
to retrieve it and find myself
sprinting back where I had been.

I am bent double trying to grasp
the tumbling tossing whirling object
and missing while dodging cars,
pedestrians, dogs, and rattling cans

rolling fast past; I leap small fences,
hop on and off curbs; finally
I pin the cap in an alley
next to a dumpster

behind my apartment building where I
had started out with such ambition
just a few minutes earlier. Out
of breath, energy, will, and interest, I lean

against a brick wall and wonder how often
I have backtracked without knowing, ending
where I set out. I realize I have enacted
the story of my life: a comedy in one act.

I collapse onto the pavement. I begin
to laugh, strangely content
to be going nowhere, at ease
with the breeze and clouds passing overhead.

(Tallinn, Estonia, Spring 2003)

CHOOSING

Each window holds a world, no two
quite the same.

Each world holds a you; choose one,
the others forever lost.

She takes your hand. You step through.
Nothing will ever be the same.

You look back. The window is gone. Look
ahead. She smiles. She waits.

Children peer round her dress. Their shy eyes
welcome you. You forget the window.

You walk to your new family. A choir
of birds sings. A road unspools into the distance.

(Tallinn, Estonia, Spring 2003)

THE BOOK OF YEARS

Leafing through it one finds
gaps, missing pages where
one expected exhaustive detail.
This is the record of one's life,
the repository of those stories
recited as though they are
mantras, litanies, well-worn prayers.
Even the most frequently visited
of these tales, however, reveal
(when looked at closely) missing

details, blurred print, misprints--
in short, coherence and meaning
fade when scrutiny intensifies.
This is the unabridged volume
of personal memory. It is where
one stores all information needed
to define who and what one is.
For years it has been the arbiter
of any doubts regarding family
or self or friends. As the years

pile one on top of the other,
the book becomes unwieldy,
hard to hold; the font size recedes
until even the strongest glasses
do not provide access to certain words.
The volume is now too large to read
in one or two or even three sittings.
Certain entries startle when one encounters
them, they describe a stranger's life, summon
no familiar images to the mind, they threaten

one's very sanity by calling into question
long held personal truths. One begins
to leave the book on its shelf for longer
and longer periods of time. Finally, one forgets
in which room one has stored the book. One delays
searching for it. A new book is started. It is written
in large print. The entries are kept simple. Only heroic
events are recorded. The old book fades. When it is
mentioned, one has no memory it ever existed.
One memorizes the new book, recites from it daily.

(Lakeport, California, 2003)

WHERE DO A POET'S WORDS COME FROM

the wind, but not borne on the wind, something
inside the wind, some feeling which suggests
possibilities, a joy and a sadness intertwined

the ocean, but not riding the waves, something
intrinsic, a force which summons song, which
compels utterance of those twins, hope and despair

the rain, but only when one stands or walks in it,
its steady commitment to grief, not the words of
grief, but the feel, the taste, the forgiveness, the prayer

the mountains, not their grandeur, rather their
endurance, their ineffable patience, their connection
of earth and sky, their challenge to rise above, to dare

(Lakeport, California, 2004)

Of Goodbyes Memories and Eidolons:
Poems from 2006-2020

WADI AND STONE

My feet surrounded by fossilized plants and sea life,
I stand in a desert wind, mind flown over wadi and stone.

In the distance is a stand of trees, green and alone. Are they
really here in a land of wadi and stone?

In some homes, there is no love, no hope for it to grow. Yet
love can appear in hearts made of wadi and stone.

Years can pass formed from rock and carved by howling
wind. Then there's a sound of water down wadi and stone.

Walking across rock, gravel, and fossils lost to time, look,
Michael, the future slips down wadi, through stone.

(Riyadh, Saudi Arabia, June 2006)

MIRACLE TAKEN FOR GRANTED

uploading files of information
to an imaginary site twelve thousand miles away

watching a sun being born
thousands of light years distant

talking casually to a friend
on the other side of the world

seeing the Andes from the air when only hours before
the only thing to be seen were the streets of Los Angeles

and the three year old forming full sentences
without formal instruction and in two languages

(Riyadh, Saudi Arabia, Spring 2007)

A TEMPORARY STAY

Apart again, breathing slips into sleep, and your hair
upon the pillow is ruffled by the wind sighing through
the opened window while the rain continues its steady

rhythm on roof and sill, and an occasional car splashes
slowly down our midnight side street. I drape a blanket
across bare thighs, tuck it under your arms, and slide

out of bed, tiptoe into the living room to read and listen
to the immense night humming at the window, the future
in all its uncertainty held at bay for a few more hours…

(Riyadh, Saudi Arabia, June 2006)

HER PARTS LIKE WATER FLOW

What grace is this
that fills the air like snow
in still December;

what movement vanishing
when touched; what beauty
sure to blind?

Tomorrow or the day
or month after,
will memory be credible?

All through the park
men and women
gaze in wonder and disbelief.

(Riyadh, Saudi Arabia, Autumn 2006)

GOING TO WORK

I slowly stroll into the early morning's light
where a pale moon, reluctant to depart,

hangs above surrounding peaks--it is a guest
who has stayed too long and now can not find

the will or words to say goodbye. Pigeons
have already invaded the side streets I walk

and are surly when shunted aside to clear a path.
An old basset hound meanders up, his head lifted,

his jowls flopping in a rhythm which suggests
a strong breeze is blowing. He moves off

when ignored, looking back over his shoulder
once or twice, as though expecting to be called back.

From the west come high clouds of the purest white,
and from the east come storm clouds. A burly German

Shepherd attacks the gate to his home and barks
with a fierce vigor while an old man nods to me

with a courtly manner and says buen dia in a hoarse voice.
Two ancient Aymara women who work outside the school

broadly smile and call me by name, even though I have yet
to learn their names. Just past the school guard shack,

I stop, take a deep breath, inhale the mountains' beauty,
and then slowly move toward another day of classes.

It feels as if I have already lived a full day, just
making the leisurely journey here. I notice the moon

has disappeared. The clouds seem to be joining.
My joints ache. Rain is on the way. I begin to sing.

(La Paz, Bolivia, December 2008)

EPIPHANY

Close to midnight there is a whisper
of rain, a low murmur of water
streaming downhill, an occasional

splashing of tires passing
along dim nearby streets;
I open a curtain, lift

my eyes to the mountains
where lightning's fierce scrawl
is written and thunder reverberates

among barely visible peaks
wrapped round in clouds and sprinkled
with faint lights winking upwards

in sprawling chains toward the Altiplano.
I suddenly realize that in this ancient
towering land, my presence is irrelevant.

Man comes and goes. The mountains
define this place. The storms inhabit it.
I am only a tourist, a passing fancy

imagined by the land and then forgotten.
All night I dream a vast sky filled with wings.
My throat fills with sound which predates man.

(La Paz, Bolivia, February 9, 2009)

OF GOODBYES MEMORIES AND EIDOLONS

As I fade into silence,
as my image becomes a mirage,
a ghost, a memory glimpsed
from the corner of your eye,

remember that you and I each
carry the other in a gesture here,
a phrase there, a sudden burst of laughter,
and we have changed one another

in ways we may never recognize,
and these mountains are our witnesses.

(La Paz, Bolivia, late May 2011)

GAVOTTE FOR A RAINY DAY

Alone, going downhill along a muddy dirt road
through a late afternoon downpour, half-drowned
but enjoying rain, rambling thoughts,
absence of cars or other people, embracing

soaked shirt and trousers, big grin on face, leaping
from dry patch to dry patch, and humming,
"Didn't it rain, children, didn't it rain," I hear a voice
offer an umbrella. I turn to see a guard for one

of the homes I am passing offer me shelter as he leans
under an overhang, umbrella in hand, a concerned look
on face. I decline graciously as an old bedraggled wet man
in driving rain can manage, and move on whistling,

enjoying the weather and the fact that a stranger
is willing to offer a haven for no apparent reason.
Thunder cracks, booms, rolls, and rebounds,
and I find a lilt, bless my Celtic ancestors, in my aged step.

(September 2011, Kigali, Rwanda)

WILD I AM SHOUTED THE OLD MAN

damn the wind and rain
I will hobble on down the road
to meet daily obligations

hello post office hello pharmacy
hello bank hello supermarket
hello the wild elation found

in windblown showers drenching me
head to toe side to side front to back
even my walking stick is slick

from non-stop downpour
my glasses are wetter than windshields
without wipers puddles explode

into my path every time a car passes
I am blinded by water to the point
I stumble over curbs and wade

through small ponds in street
on sidewalk on roadside
eventually a passing truck

drapes me in curtains of water
and I discover myself laughing
with a mad exuberance I have not felt

since boyhood frolics playing
football and basketball
on muddy fields puddle-filled

and storm drenched
suddenly I am singing "didn't
it rain children rain all night long"

and I dance a clumsy dance
of an old fool who does not
know enough to get out of the rain

my body which has long abandoned
me to the limitations of gravity
decides to reclaim the enthusiasm

of youth for a minute for five minutes
for a time not measurable for jubilation
unrestrained a kind of drunkenness

long lost and most welcome a corporeal jazz
a music of the soul unlimited a prayer
that every living minute be felt and celebrated

(Reedsport, Oregon, July 2019)

SOME JIVE

(for Joseph Glaser)

I walk miles each day to stay alive.
Despite your doubts, this is no jive.

Walking past rivers and creeks, I see
herons, otters, ducks, and deer -- no jive.

Ambling into the library frees me
from noise of traffic, trains, and all that jive.

Midnight walks remove people from view,
and I relax, freed from all that jive.

We used to talk, rambling rap, for hours
on midnight street corners. We really jived.

Admit it Newell, your mouth and feet both
love to ramble. I tell the truth. No jive.

(Reedsport, Oregon, February 2015)

SPECTATOR SPORTS

The road past my residence is a river
of people of all ages (solo, in pairs,
in large groups), goods (fruits, vegetables,
dresses, shirts, chairs, tables, tools,

and whatever else can be carried by
hand, on wrist, arm, shoulder, head,
or draped or wrapped around neck),
motos carrying or seeking passengers,

cars (small, large, expensive, cheap,
new, battered), and a cornucopia
of sound (conversation soft and loud,
shouts up and down the dirt street--

often filled with mud--between friends
and family members, songs solo
and in groups large and small,
roosters crowing, goats bleating,

horns announcing the presence of vehicles),
and I lean against a railing street side
to watch and listen and smile at
the astonishing variety of uninhibited life

which enriches me even as I measure
out my days as an abiding watcher,
one who finds joy in the unabashed
vigor and ebullience and daring of others.

(Kigali, Rwanda, 2011-2014)

REMEMBERING
(for Pungo, r.i.p. 2007)

I still feel his frail bones, hear his kind words, remember
(as we parted) his loving, spectral touch, my silence.
On my refrigerator is a picture of him and my mother,

smiling into the future and the raising of family,
faces unlined, no gray in hair, a fearless acceptance
in eyes for what might come. My mind adjusts,

recalls boyhood and the two people in the photo,
decades wiped away, the long journey just begun
which would end in a trailer with him in great pain

held in my mother's and brother's arms, while I returned
to a job as a surrogate parent for rich people's children
in a foreign land. I would seek forgiveness, if I knew

from whom and for what. When I look at the photo,
I hear whispers whose words I can not quite distinguish.
I imagine movement and think someone is about to walk

into the picture, a brother, a sister, me, and realize
I am still alone, still silent, still draped in confusion,
unable to reach through time, and seek a blessing.

(Kigali, Rwanda, January 2012)

**WANDERING THROUGH MEMORY'S BACK
ALLEYS**

Live enough places and nowhere
is home, but everywhere
one meets people
who live for decades
in head and heart.

Certain incidents never fade:
the dog wearing a helmet,
jaws clamped onto a cigar,
ensconced on back
of a motorcycle, while

the rider in jeans and t-shirt,
in the middle of a snowstorm,
waves cheerfully at
bemused bystanders waiting
for a bus or trolley car;

one cabbie bellows
imprecations at grinning
cyclist and imperturbable dog,
I shake my head,
but can not stop laughing.

There was a cafe in Tashkent,
run by a Turk, whose cooks were
Korean, bartenders Russian, waitresses
Russian, Estonian, Tajik, and Tartar,
and customers from all over Europe,

North America, and most parts of Asia,
a cafe whose food mixed Turkish,
French, and Russian cuisine, whose
music was provided by Gypsy, Israeli,
and Russian musicians who played

everything from Bob Dylan to Paul Simon,
Irish folk music to Oscar Peterson,
Mussorgsky to Doc Watson, Turkish
songs to Hava Nageela, the Bach-Gounod
Ave Maria to Creedence Clearwater Revival.

When I left town, the cafe's staff collected funds
to buy me an inscribed pocket watch, complete
with chain, with my name misspelled on the back,
an expensive gift for people living on twenty
(or fewer) dollars per month. I was told

it was an antique. The watch stopped
running in a week. I still have it and read
the inscription several times a year.
The watch is valued as an old daguerreotype
might have been decades ago -- it contains

a tangible history, history
that floats through dreams on rainy coastal
Oregon small town nights
in this dimly lit apartment where I muse
and write about the past, a past

more vibrant than my daily life.
Once on a side street in La Paz,
I sprinted across cobblestone, to avoid
delaying an oncoming car
packed with multiple generations of a family,

and I tripped on the curb as I reached
the other side and fell flat on my face,
spilling books from my backpack
across street and sidewalk; the car emptied
its eight or so occupants and all helped me

to my feet; a woman in her eighties took
a pristine handkerchief from a purse
and wiped my bloody face, three sets
of hands probed me for broken
bones; offers to drive me anywhere

were tendered in Spanish and English.
I thanked everyone, assured them I was fine,
and went on my way, only to encounter
them five minutes later in a large
grocery store where everyone re-examined

me to reassure themselves of my well-being.
Such graciousness appears again and again
in my travels. In Tallinn I slipped on black ice
on a very snowy day, but before I could
tumble into the banks of snow along the street,

a small hand grabbed my elbow, helped
me regain my balance, and I glanced down
to discover a small Russian woman in her early
eighties patting my arm and inquiring if I was
alright. I assured her I was okay, and off she sped

at twice the speed I could muster on those
icy, snowy, barely visible streets at six-thirty
in the morning. In a very different land,
one Americans often bemoan, there was a little
watch repairman and his wife who saved me

from my ineptitude and inability to follow directions --
I was in Monterrey, Mexico; I stumbled
into their small shop on a back street
completely lost and knowing no one. Neither
husband nor wife spoke much English and

my Spanish was little better. He figured out
where I was trying to reach, left his shop
to his wife's care, even though he had
several customers waiting, led me down
two blocks and around a corner where

he found a taxi, and ensured that
the driver knew where to take me;
the little fellow refused payment,
his graciousness as intrinsic,
as taken for granted, as breathing.

There was a Syrian barber in Kuwait
who stopped during the middle of every
haircut, no matter how many people were
waiting, to take a tea break and offer
baklava, currants, dates, and

an assortment of cookies; he spoke no English,
my Arabic was but a few words, yet
he talked and laughed and patted my arm
for five or ten minutes before resuming
the haircut -- which was always done well.

In Cairo I once asked directions
of two men leaning against
a barbershop. They argued with one
another in Arabic, seemed to reach agreement,
and began to give me directions in English.

No sooner had they begun than a crowd
of middle-aged men, dressed both in European
and Middle-Eastern garb joined them
from the barber shop and nearby small market.
A heated discussion ensued which eventually

culminated in ten sets of hands pointing in
ten different directions, lots of loud disagreement,
then smiles and everyone left. I stood there
in utter bafflement until a lad, who
had watched the entire soap opera, took me

around the corner, up one street and pointed
to my destination. I thanked him profusely,
and asked why he had not intervened sooner.
He said the show had been too good to miss,
so he had waited until it was over.

Certain themes appear and reappear along
memory's streets: being lost in one's own
neighborhood until eventually, hours late,
arriving home, usually with the assistance
of a stranger. This happened in Mexico,

Egypt, Estonia, Rwanda, Kuwait, Abu Dhabi,
Bolivia, Jordan, and Uzbekistan. The circumstances
are almost always the same; I go for a walk,
decide to visit a side street, and suddenly find
myself caught in loops which lead nowhere.

I have decided this is my life: loops leading nowhere,
yet always leading me home. This is as true
of my life choices (whether romantic or
professional), as it is of my peripatetic wanderings
through back alleys of a dozen nations.

One constant in expat life
is trusting strangers, accepting
that my well-being is often
in the hands of people and occasions
beyond my ability to control.

There is a joy that comes from wandering
unknown neighborhoods, talking to anyone
inclined to chat, drifting with life's
ebb and flow through places never before
frequented and not necessarily understood,

such as walking in on a wedding
celebration in a Cairo hotel courtyard,
and being invited to watch, eat, drink,
dance if I were so inclined, and clap along
with the wedding party to Arabic dance music.

The joy and abandon of that wedding
has infused my thoughts for years.
Such events inform my words, whether written
or spoken, whenever I have occasion to remember.
More importantly, such events remind me

to be alert to events in my every day life.
Whenever I find myself sinking in the mire
of petty despondency, I remember that wedding,
a midnight sky in La Paz, walking with friends
on the Corniche in Abu Dhabi, being lost

for miles in a gully in Monterrey and coming
upon young lovers amidst wandering donkeys
and one stray horse (and the lovers bestowing
on me shy smiles and directions to where
I could leave the gully), and a Gypsy guitarist

(who claimed he once backed Doc Watson
in Moscow) playing bluegrass in a Tashkent
restaurant while a Jewish Russian vocalist
sang old mountain music lyrics in a heavy
Russian accent while she strummed rhythm guitar.

All these incidents remind me that
astonishment and joy are everywhere,
but to find such moments I must be alert,
aware of wonders that teem on every street,
in every alley. To be alert, to welcome possibility,

to dare, these are gifts of a life led among strangers;
I would be a boor not to acknowledge
that strangers have enriched my days
with amazement, laughter, and comfort. I tip
my hat to distant voices and laughter on the wind.

(Reedsport, Oregon, November 2018)

LIBIAMO LIBIAMO

His walk, a clock slowing
in its arc toward stillness,

clumps awkwardly in dissolution's
direction without awareness

of anything but where the next
step will be placed to avoid

stumble, tumble, or face first dive.
He hums the brindisi from *La Traviata*

and surprises himself with a slow
pirouette which ends with him leaning

against a wall, smiling, and waving on
the young couple who stopped nearby

in concern for his well-being; being touched
by their awkward desire to help, he thanks them,

and lurches in their wake, silently laughing,
and wondering if it is possible

to be intoxicated by song lyrics. A cold sun
lights his path homeward. He resumes humming.

(Reedsport, Oregon, December 30, 2014)

FOR A MADCAP FOOL OF GRACE WIT AND CHARM

(for Jonathan McMurtry)

Ah, Jonathan, wounded air whispers your name,
recites the long roll call of all the roles
you have blessed with your imagination,
passion, unique voice, and wicked daring
that informed all characters you brought
into the sacramental presence of the theatre,
where you lifted thousands of witnesses
over the years into flights of fancy, wild outbursts

of laughter, tears mourning life's losses,
and overwhelming truths they took home
to bless their lives for years to come.
Your generosity welcomed dozens and dozens
of young actors into the theatre over the decades.
You rigorously plied your craft from your days
(hard to believe) when you were an apprentice
through your days as a journeyman into

the many years you were a master of your trade.
I still see you, drink in hand, hours after
a performance had ended, with a host of young
actors gathered round you, laughing at your
thousand and one tales of great actors, their gifts,
their foibles, their eccentricities, their achievements,
their gusto for life, a gusto you shared with them,
and with the young men and women gathered round

you to hear your tales of the men and women
who made theatre worth doing, worth living.
You lived to bring to life the wild imaginings
of great writers across the centuries, to swim
the river uniting men and women of the theatre
from Thespis to the present, to add to theatre's
rich tapestries your own unique insight and depth
of feeling and intellect, given freely and bounteously.
As I sit here, in the very early hours of the morning,
tears come unbidden, remembering you as Claudius,
looking at pictures of you in dozens of different
roles in as many different theatres, lamenting
the fact I never told you how special I thought
you were as man and actor. Late at night,
in theatres across the land, your presence
still alive, even though your body has left us,

causes the air to ripple in remembrance.
For however many years I have left, I will
remember you whenever I pass a theatre,
and imagine I could go in after midnight,
and all alone see you performing all the roles
in Hamlet or the Scottish play or bringing
Chekhov alive for an audience of one.
Jonathan, you are remembered, and you live

as long as the hundreds of actors you have
touched over the years share stories of you
and learned from you, and as long as those
who came to your performances remember,
you live and we are richer for it. For many of us
who met you while we were young, you
have been our Thespis, the one who led us
into the rites of the theatre, who anointed us

into performances' rituals. Pax vobiscum.
As I finish my night's work on this poem,
early morning light creeps over nearby hills,
and I hear your elven voice whisper in my ears,
you know you could do better with this poem --
if not for me, then for the poem. Your work
is never done. There is always more to be found.
I mutter thank you old friend for the reminder.

(Reedsport, Oregon, July 17, 2019)

WANDERING

Under a warm African sky, I wandered for miles
in every direction near the motel where I lived,
traversing semi-rural Kigali side streets of cracked,
cratered mud looping deep into valleys filled with
huts and agricultural fields, hopping over crevices,
strolling through long gullies carved by trucks
and large cars during rainy seasons, gullies pockmarked
by stones large, medium, small, and almost invisible,
keeping one eye on the path underfoot while the other
roamed over huts, humble churches, open fields,

pedestrians of every size and shape, a beautiful
rough hewn world of chaotic order -- children playing
soccer and begging for money, adults leaning against
walls of small shops staring curiously at this strange
foreigner wandering alone through their midst, some
scowling, many more smiling, a few trying out their
English, others calling greetings in Kinyarwanda,
chickens running freely through the streets, a group
of geese spending nearly a month on one corner
near a large puddle that took weeks to dry up, a puddle

gleefully invaded with utter abandon by small children
swinging sticks and chasing squawking birds who resettled
into place as soon as the children wandered off,
stopping now and again I listened to a cappella gospel
singing coming from churches and homes packed
with small gatherings whose voices would rise
at unexpected times for hours of fervent shouts
and songs which slowed my walk (at times to a full
halt), and inevitably I would get lost for hours
before stumbling on the right path home.

The whole experience I have come to believe
is a metaphor for my life and how I have lived it,
staggering from day to day and week to week
trusting blindly that the world means me no harm
beyond that contained in the limitation of days
I am provided about which I can do little except
fill them with constant surprise and the hope of more
surprises appearing near and far, around the corner
and on the horizon, and accepting these gifts
(which occasionally are not desired) with equanimity.

(Reedsport, Oregon, March 2015)

THEN AND NOW

Many years past I sat against a wall,
stared across boulevards, rows of houses
and apartment buildings, toward distant hills

draped in a soft rain and a sun falling
toward evening, and wondered what awaited
down the decades before me; when and where

would I end up, what would I do and not do,
what places and people would come into
my life and change me and how and who;

and how would I change who and what lay before me;
I leaned against that wall on a college campus
and imagined dozens of scenarios, few of which

ever appeared even briefly, and none which
ever became significant; yet still on a day blurred
by a steady rain, I remember that late afternoon

where I envisioned with great feeling a life
that never happened, and in memory I find myself
back there looking ahead with the same excitement

that gripped me some fifty years ago, still imagining
dozens of life paths, even though the reality is
my life is simply putting one foot in front of the other,

and slowly moving along whatever path has presented
itself; grateful to have a path, and feet
that will still stumble ahead one step at a time,

and a mind that is amused by its encounters,
and a heart still capable of loving life's oddities,
its surprises, its baffling contradictions; and willing

to continue being open to a world never understood,
but frequently capable of evoking wild surmise
and hope, yes, always that beautiful nugget, hope.

(Reedsport, Oregon, September 2019)

METAMORPHOSIS

One final time the old man erases the blackboard,
casually dismisses the class he has taught
for the last three years, and then collapses

into a chair to watch his life disappear out the door;
one or two students shake hands and wish him well
before hurrying out the door to waiting cars

and summer vacation. He is uncertain where
he goes from here, or whether he will ever hear
from the vanishing students, but it does not matter.

He has done all he can and begins to plan
his future, the few years between now
and the dark tunnel approaching ever nearer

day by day, a gaping maw about which he knows
nothing save his fear of nothingness. He glances
at the door through which the focus of his energy

for the last several decades has vanished.
He stands and leaves the cocoon of the classroom
for one last time on his way to nowhere

in particular where he will have time to think
and write and begin to discover himself
or some reasonable approximation.

A butterfly lands on his shoulder. He brushes it off,
but it returns, not once, but twice. He accepts
its presence, but eventually a gust lifts it

into erratic flight. Erratic flight -- the old man
smiles at the thought. That has been the story
of his life, wildly veering paths which have

brought him here to a precipice where he
will shortly begin his freefall toward remaining days
which summon him to discovery, despair, or wild surprise.

(Kigali, Rwanda, June 2014)

LET US NOW GIVE THANKS FOR

the deer and hare, the fox
and crow, the wind
and rain, the thunder's roll,
the night in mist, the sweep
of snow, delicate balance
of the hurricane's eye, the cry
of the lark in the morning.

Michael L. Newell was born in Florida in 1945. In addition to living in thirteen states, he has lived in Japan, The Philippine Islands, Thailand, The United Arab Emirates, Jordan, Kuwait, Uzbekistan, Mexico, Egypt, Estonia, Saudi Arabia, Bolivia, and Rwanda. He currently lives in a small town on the Florida coast.

Newell studied writing with Benjamin Saltman and Ann Stanford. His poems have appeared in a number of periodicals including *Aethlon: The Journal of Sport Literature; Bellowing Ark; College English; Current; English Journal; First Class; The Iconoclast; Issa's Untidy Hut; Jerry Jazz Musician; Lilliput Review; Poetry Depth Quarterly; Rattle; Shemom; Ship of Fools; Tulane Review; and Verse-Virtual.*

Some of his previous books include *A Stranger to the Land; Seeking Shelter; A Long Time Traveling; Traveling without Compass or Map; and Meditation of an Old Man Standing on a Bridge.*

www.ingramcontent.com/pod-product-compliance
Lightning Source LLC
LaVergne TN
LVHW091111180726
843490LV00002B/730